SECRET SPELLS
&
CURIOUS CHARMS

Also by Monika Beisner
MONIKA BEISNER'S BOOK OF RIDDLES
A FOLDING ALPHABET BOOK
AN ADDRESS BOOK

And with Alison Lurie
THE HEAVENLY ZOO
FABULOUS BEASTS

Monika Beisner

SECRET SPELLS & CURIOUS CHARMS

JONATHAN CAPE
THIRTY-TWO BEDFORD SQUARE LONDON

For my mother

First published 1985
Illustrations copyright © 1985 by Monika Beisner
Jonathan Cape Ltd, 32 Bedford Square, London WC1B 3EL

British Library Cataloguing in Publication Data

Beisner, Monika
Secret spells and curious charms.
1. Charms   2. Incantations
I. Title
133.4'4   BF1561

ISBN 0-224-02282-2

The text on pp. 6–7, 18–19 and 30–1, slightly adapted, is taken from *The Secret
Lore of Magic* by Idries Shah, published by Frederick Muller Limited, London.
"White horse, white horse," p. 12, "If you stand on a line," p. 28, and
"Pinkety, pinkety," p. 32, are reprinted from *The Lore and Language of Schoolchildren*
by Iona and Peter Opie (1959) by permission of Oxford University Press

Printed in Italy by Amilcare Pizzi S.p.A., Milano

I'll go to the toad
That lives under the wall;
I'll charm him out
And he'll come to my call.

To travel from one place to another
by flying as fast as the fastest hawk:

take snow and boil it with oil
on a fire of two kinds of wood
(one white, the other red).
Then put the mixture in a bag
made from a sheep's bladder.
When this has been in the bladder
for a moon and a half,
pour it over charcoal,
and when it is all mixed together
pound it to powder on an alabaster table.

Keep this powder in a horn.
When you want to fly, take a pinch of the powder
and place it within the pages of a book.

Put the book in your robe
in a pocket which has been prepared for it.

Then take the book, sit with it in your hand,
and think of the place to which you are to fly.
At first this will take you a long time.
When you are ready to fly and feel tired, then you must say
"SISPI, SISPI",
and you will instantly be at your destination.

When you want to return home, you must say
"ITTSS, ITTSS",
and you will be back.

One for sorrow,
Two for joy,
Three for a girl,
Four for a boy,
Five for silver,
Six for gold,
Seven for a secret
Never to be told.

Three white stones,
And three black pins,
Three yellow daisies
From the green.
Into the well
With a one, two, three,
A fortune, a fortune,
Come to me.

Look to the moon when she is round,
Luck with you shall then abound;
What you seek for shall be found,
In sea or sky or solid ground.

White horse, white horse,
Bring me good luck.
Good luck to you,
Good luck to me,
Good luck to everyone I see.

Even ash, I thee do pluck,
Hoping thus to meet good luck.
If no luck I get from thee,
I'll wish I'd left you on the tree.

See a pin and pick it up,
All the day you'll have good luck.
See a pin and let it lay,
Bad luck you will have all day.

Who kills a spider,
Bad luck betides her.

The sparrow and the redbreast,
The martin and the swallow:
If you touch one of their eggs,
Bad luck is sure to follow.

You must break the shell to bits, for fear
The witches make it a boat, my dear:
For over the sea, away from home,
Far by night the witches roam.

Flibberty, gibberty, flasky flum,
Calafa, tarada, wagra wum.
Hooky, maroosky, whatever's the sum,
Heigho! Presto! Money come!

To be revenged upon one who has done you harm:

say RAIZINO seven times
to the points of the compass,
when you are alone after nightfall.

Then take a blue pencil,
and write this square
upon a dried, triangular leaf:

When the leaf is complete,
it must be burnt in a lamp flame
which has not been outside
for more than three hours at a time.

And there must be no other person
within three hundred paces of you
when you work.
It is best to do this
in a place which no one visits,
and always to carry with you
a quantity of black cord,
tied around your right arm.

The fig tree is her staff, folks say;
Destroy it not in any way.
Upon it lies a dreadful curse,
Who plucks a leaf will need a hearse.

You must search the meadows over
Till you find a four-leafed clover:
Fortune then will smile on you,
Make your dearest wish come true.

Beware of that man,
Be he friend or brother,
Whose hair is one colour
And moustache another.

He loves me,
He don't.
He'll have me,
He won't.
He would
If he could.
But he can't
So he don't.

I place my shoes like a letter T,
Hoping my true love I shall see;
What he is and what he wears,
And what he does all months and years.

The fair maid who, the first of May,
Goes to the fields at break of day,
And washes in dew
From the hawthorn tree,
Will ever after handsome be.

Right cheek! Left cheek!
Why do you burn?
Right cheek for love,
And left cheek for spite.
But either side
Is good at night.

Find an odd-leafed ash
And an even-leafed clover,
And you'll see your true love
Before the day is over.

If your horse has four white legs,
Keep him not a day;
If your horse has three white legs,
Send him far away;
If your horse has two white legs,
Sell him to a friend;
But if your horse has one white leg,
Keep him to the end.

If you stand on a line,
You'll marry a swine;
If you stand on a square,
You'll marry a bear.

To cause love between two people:
take three strings, one each for the colours of
the earth, the sun and the moon.

These are placed tied together
in a small jar or earthenware pot.
When they have lain there for six days,
add a little juice of the jasmine flower.

Press all together. From this will be made an ink,
which is to be used to write the square.
Then take a piece of white cloth
that has been steeped in barley water and dried.
Write the square upon this cloth with the ink.
The square is to be written at the first hour of day,
when you can just see.
It is better to wait in the dark,
with everything ready, until such time
as you are able to see clearly.

Then start to write the square.
It is as follows:

And when this square is complete,
place it between two flat stones in your room.

When it has been there for two nights more,
take it out, and say to it in a loud voice
the names of the two people who are to love each other.
Repeat this for another three days.
Then what you wish will be accomplished.

Pinkety, pinkety, thumb to thumb,
Wish a wish and it's sure to come;
If yours comes true,
Mine will come true,
Pinkety, pinkety, thumb to thumb.